may
you
walk
with
a
piece
of
sunlight
always
in
your
heart.

This Journal Belongs to:

As we become aware of all of the wondrous experiences that occur in our lives, we begin to recognize that beauty, joy, laughter and gratitude are available to us every moment.

Here is a sacred place for you to record your thoughts, express your feelings, write poetry and acknowledge all the special gifts that each day brings.

Renée Locks is an artist, writer, calligrapher and poet who expresses her love of nature through the delicate strokes and swirls of her sumi brush.

Just
Trust
yourself.
Then
you
will
Know
how
To
Live.
.GOETHE

When your
HEART
speaks,
Take
good
notes.

Life
is
a
great
bundle
of
little
Things

O W HOLMES

Let us not look back
in Anger
or forward
in Fear
but
Around
in
Awareness.

JAMES THURBER

forward, forward,
Let us not disappoint
The moon before us.

may you walk with a piece of sunlight
always in your heart.

Let us live
The HIGHEST VISION
of what is possible.

INGA GRACE

Each day provides its own gifts.

Life is either
A DARING
adventure
or
nothing.

HELEN
KELLER

If a tree can grow
from such a little seed
what can our hearts
become in our long
journey toward the stars

We who whittle ourselves to suit everybody

will soon whittle ourselves away

I get up.
I walk.
I fall
down.

Meanwhile,
I keep
Dancing.

why
not
go
out
on a
Limb?
Isn't
That
where
The
fruit
is?

the heart must have
its time of snow:
to rest
in silence
and then
to grow

We cannot direct the wind

but we can adjust our sails.

I was always looking
outside myself
for strength
and confidence
but it comes from
within; it is
there all the
time.

/ ANNA
FREUD

Remember
four simple
words:
LIVE
LOVE
LAUGH
BLOOM

The challenge
is to be
yourself
in a
world
that is
trying
to
make
you
like
everyone
else

May
I
live
Simply
That
others
may
Simply
live

·

GANDHI

May
your
life
be like
a wildflower
growing
freely
in the
beauty
and joy
of each
day.

· INDIAN PROVERB

Fall down
Seven
Times.
Get up
Eight !

JAPANESE
PROVERB

To keep our faces toward change and behave like free spirits

in the presence of fate is strength undefeatable.   HELEN
                                                     KELLER

Have
patience
with
all things,
but,
first of all,
with
yourself.

We bless Life
by Dancing

LET me be
JOY,
be
HOPE;
LET
my
life
SING.

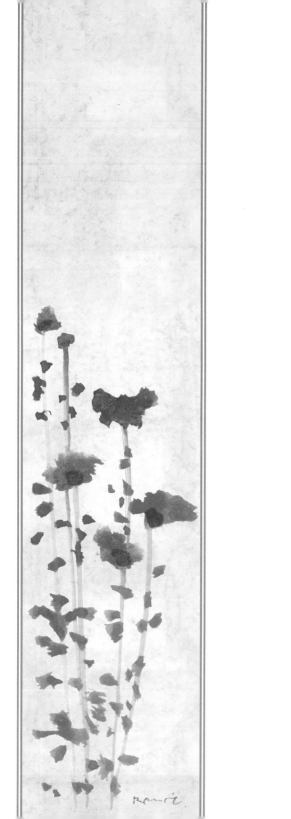

Let
the
beauty
we
love
be
what
we
do.

'SUFI'

Sing, Laugh,
do
as you
wish
say

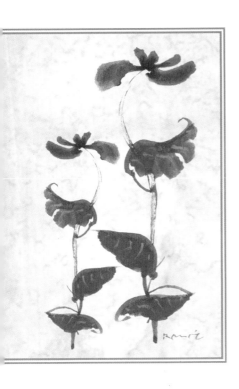

Be patient
dear heart,
Life's plans,
like Lilies,
pure and
white
unfold.

MAY
RILEY
SMITH

As the sun illuminates the moon and the stars

So let us illuminate each other. MISTER LUI

. . . and then the day came when the risk to remain tight in a bud was more painful than the risk it took to blossom.

— ANAÏS NIN

LET the Butterflies
come to you

Accept the gift
you have given
to so many.
Let people
love you back.

Jeanette
Osias

IF WE ONLY LOOK DOWN, THERE WILL NEVER BE STARS.

HAKUIN

my desire is
throughout
the four seasons
to remember
to enjoy them
and to not let
a day pass
without some
flower opening

I get up.
I walk.
I fall
down.

Meanwhile,
I keep
Dancing.

may
your
Troubles
be less;
your
Happiness
more
and
nothing
but
Blessings
come
Through
your
Door.

Renée Locks is a multi-media artist, calligrapher and poet.
Through words and art, Renée creates designs that nourish,
heal and bless the mind, heart and spirit.

All Artwork by Renée Locks.
Book design by Liz Kalloch.